A Special Gift

For

_____

From

_____

Date

_____

Message

_____

_____

Fragrance

of

Hope

~ Helen Steiner Rice ~

Fleming H. Revell
A Division of Baker Book House Co
Grand Rapids, Michigan 49516

Good Morning, God!

You are ushering in another day
untouched and freshly new
here I come to ask You, God,
You'll renew me, too,
forgive the many errors
that I made yesterday
and let me try again, dear God,
to walk closer in Thy way ...
but, Father, I am well aware
I can't make it on my own
so take my hand and hold it tight
for I can't walk alone!

It's Me Again, God

Remember me, God?
I come every day
Just to talk with You, Lord,
And to learn how to pray ...
You make me feel welcome,
You reach out Your hand,
I need never explain
For You understand ...
I come to You frightened
And burdened with care
So lonely and lost
And so filled with despair,
And suddenly, Lord,
I'm no longer afraid,
My burden is lighter
And the dark shadows fade ...
Oh, God, what a comfort
To know that You care
And to know when I seek You
You will always be there!

Daily Prayers Are "Heaven's Stairs"

The "Stairway" rises "Heaven high" –
The "steps" are dark and steep,
In weariness we climb them
As we stumble, fall, and weep ...
And many times we falter
Along the "path of prayer"
Wondering if You hear us
And if You really care ...
Oh, give us some assurance,
Restore our faith anew,
So we can keep on climbing
The "Stairs of Prayer" to You –
For we are weak and wavering,
Uncertain and unsure,
And only meeting You in prayer
Can help us to endure
All life's trials and troubles
Its sickness, pain, and sorrow,
And give us strength and courage
To face and meet tomorrow!

What Is Prayer?

Is it measured words that are memorized,
Forcefully said and dramatized,
Offered with pomp and with arrogant pride
In words unmatched to the feelings inside?
No ... prayer is so often just words unspoken
Whispered in tears by a heart that is broken ...
For God is already deeply aware
Of the burdens we find too heavy to bear,
And all we need do is to seek Him in prayer
And without a word He will help us to bear
Our trials and troubles – our sickness and sorrow
And show us the way to a brighter tomorrow ...
There's no need at all for impressive prayer
For the minute we seek God He is already there!

God, Are You There?

I'm way down here!
You're way up there!
Are You sure You can hear
My faint, faltering prayer?
For I'm so unsure
Of just how to pray –
To tell you the truth, God,
I don't know what to say ...
I just know I am lonely
And vaguely disturbed,
Bewildered and restless,
Confused and perturbed ...
And they tell me that prayer
Helps to quiet the mind
And to unburden the heart
For in stillness we find
A newborn assurance
That Someone does care
And Someone does answer
Each small sincere prayer!

The Mystery Of Prayer

Beyond that which words can interpret
Or theology can explain
The soul feels a "shower of refreshment"
That falls like the gentle rain
On hearts that are parched with problems
And are searching to find the way
To somehow attract God's attention
Through well-chosen words as they pray,
Not knowing that God in His wisdom
Can sense all man's worry and woe
For there is nothing man can conceal
That God does not already know ...
So kneel in prayer in His presence
And you'll find no need to speak
For softly in silent communion
God grants you the peace that you seek.

No Favor Do I Seek Today

I come not to ask, to plead, or implore You,
I just come to tell You how much I adore You,
For to kneel in Your Presence makes me feel blest
For I know that You know all my needs best ...
And it fills me with joy just to linger with You
As my soul You replenish and my heart You renew,
For prayer is much more than just asking for things –
It's the Peace and Contentment that Quietness brings ...
So thank You again for Your mercy and love
And for making me heir to Your Kingdom above!

Finding Faith In A Flower

Sometimes when faith is running low
And I cannot fathom why things are so ...
I walk alone among the flowers I grow
And learn the "answers" to all I would know!
For among my flowers I have come to see
Life's miracle and its mystery ...
And standing in silence and reverie
My faith comes flooding back to me!

God, Grant Me The Glory Of "Thy Gift"

God, widen my vision so I may see
the afflictions You have sent to me –
Not as a cross too heavy to wear
that weighs me down in gloomy despair –
Not as something to hate and despise
but as a *gift of love* sent in disguise –
Something to draw me closer to You
to teach me patience and forbearance, too –
Something to show me more clearly the way
to *serve* You and *love* You more every day –
Something priceless and precious and rare
that will keep me forever *safe* in Thy *care*
Aware of the spiritual strength that is mine
if my selfish, small will is lost in Thine!

"What Has Been Is What Will Be ... And There Is Nothing New Under The Sun" (Ecclesiastes 1:9)

Today my soul is reaching out
For something that's unknown,
I cannot grasp or fathom it
For it's known to God alone –
I cannot hold or harness it
Or put it into form,
For it's as uncontrollable
As the wind before the storm –
I know not where it came from
Or whither it will go,
For it's as inexplicable
As the restless winds that blow –
And like the wind it too will pass
And leave nothing more behind
Than the "memory of a mystery"
That blew across my mind –

t like the wind it will return

keep reminding me

at everything that has been

what again will be –

r there is nothing that is new

neath God's timeless sun,

d present, past, and future

e all molded into one –

d east and west and north and south

e same wind keeps on blowing,

hile rivers run on endlessly

t the sea's not overflowing –

d the restless unknown longing

my searching soul won't cease

til God comes in glory

d my soul at last finds peace.

Don't Let Me Falter

Oh Lord, don't let me falter –
Don't let me lose my way;
Don't let me cease to carry
My burden, day by day
Oh Lord, don't let me stumble –
Don't let me fall or quit
Oh Lord, please help me find my "job"
And help me shoulder it.

Make Me A Channel Of Blessing Today

"Make me a channel of blessing today",
I ask again and again when I pray …
Do I turn a deaf ear to the Master's voice
Or refuse to heed His directions and choice?
I only know at the end of the day
That I did so little to *"Pay my way!"*

The Answer

In the tiny petal
of a tiny flower
that grew from a tiny pod ...

is the miracle
and the mystery
of all creation and God!

God, Are You Really Real?

I want to believe
I want to be true
I want to be loyal
And faithful to You,
But where can I go
When vague doubts arise
And when "evil" appears
In an "Angel's disguise"
While clamoring voices
Demand my attention
And the air is polluted
With cries of dissension,
You know, God, it's easy
Just to follow the crowd

o are "doing their thing"
ile shouting out loud
ss protestations
inst the "old rules"
t limit and hamper
new freedom schools ...
l, answer this prayer
l tell me the truth –
You really the God
both Age and Youth?
l, God, speak to my heart
truly feel
t "these prophets" are false
You really are real!

Open My Eyes

God, open my eyes
 so I may see
And feel Your presence
 close to me ...
Give me strength
 for my stumbling feet
As I battle the crowd
 on life's busy street,
And widen the vision
 of my unseeing eyes
So in passing faces
 I'll recognize

t just a stranger,
     unloved and unknown,
t a friend with a heart
     that is much like my own ...
ve me perception
     to make me aware
at scattered profusely
     on life's thoroughfare
e the best gifts of God
     that we daily pass by
we look at the world
     with an unseeing eye.

Not To Seek, Lord, But To Share

Dear God, much too often
    we seek You in prayer
Because we are wallowing
    in our own self-despair
We make every word
    we lamentingly speak
An imperative plea
    for whatever we seek
We pray for ourselves
    and so seldom for others,
We're concerned with our problems
    and not with our brother's
We seem to forget, Lord,
    that the "sweet hour or prayer"

Is not for self-seeking
　　but to place in Your care
All the lost souls
　　unloved and unknown
And to keep praying for them
　　until they're Your own
For it's never enough
　　to seek God in prayer
With no thought of others
　　who are lost in despair
So teach us, dear God,
　　that the Power of Prayer
Is made stronger by placing
　　the world in Your care!

You Helped Us Before, God, Help Us Again

"O GOD, OUR HELP IN AGES PAST,
OUR HOPE IN YEARS TO BE" –
Look down upon this present
And see our need of Thee ...
For in this age of unrest,
With danger all around,
We need Thy hand to lead us
To higher, safer ground ...
We need Thy help and counsel
To make us more aware
That our safety and security

Lie solely in Thy care ...
Give us strength and courage
To be honorable and true
Practicing Your precepts
In everything we do,
And keep us gently humble
In the greatness of Thy love
So someday we are fit to dwell
With Thee in Peace above.

Thank God For Little Things

Thank You, God, for little things
that often come our way –
The things we take for granted
but don't mention when we pray –
The unexpected courtesy,
the thoughtful, kindly deed –
A hand reached out to help us
in the time of sudden need –
Oh, make us more aware, dear God,
of little daily graces
That come to us with "sweet surprise"
from never-dreamed-of places.

Teach Us To Live

God of love – Forgive! Forgive!
Teach us how to truly live,
Ask us not our race or creed,
Just take us in our hour of need,
And let us know You love us, too,
And that we are a part of You ...
And someday may man realize
That all the earth, the seas, and skies
Belong to God who made us all,
The rich, the poor, the great, the small,
And in the Father's Holy Sight
No man is yellow, black, or white,
And peace on earth cannot be found
Until we meet on common ground
And every man becomes a brother
Who worships God and loves all others.

Life Is Forever: Death Is A Dream!

If we did not go to sleep at night
We'd never awaken to see the light
And the joy of watching a new day break
Or meeting the dawn by some quiet lake
Would never be ours unless we slept
While God and all His angels kept
A vigil through this "little death"
That's over with the morning's breath –
And death, too, is a time of sleeping
For those who die are in God's keeping
And there's a "sunrise" for each soul
For Life not death is God's promised goal –
So trust God's promise and doubt Him never
For only through death can man live forever!

My Garden Of Prayer

My garden beautifies my yard
and adds fragrance to the air ...
But it is also my cathedral
and my quiet place of prayer ...
So little do we realize
that "The Glory and The Power"
Of He who made the universe
lies hidden in a flower.

When Troubles Assail You,
God Will Not Fail You

When life seems empty
And there's no place to go,
When your heart is troubled
And your spirits are low,
When friends seem few
And nobody cares
There is always God
To hear your prayers —
And whatever you're facing
Will seem much less
When you go to God
And confide and confess,
For the burden that seems
Too heavy to bear

lifts away
he wings of prayer –
seen through God's eyes
ly troubles diminish
we're given new strength
ce and to finish
s daily tasks
hey come along
pray for strength
eep us strong –
o to Our Father
en troubles assail you
His grace is sufficient
He'll never fail you.

I Do Not Go Alone

If death should beckon me with outstretched hand
And whisper softly of an unknown land
I shall not be afraid to go
For though the path I do not know,
I take death's hand without a fear,
For He who safely brought me here
Will also take me safely back.
And though in many things I lack,
He will not let me go alone
Into the "Valley that's unknown" ...
So I reach out and take death's hand
And journey to the *"Promised Land"*.
Kings and kingdoms all pass away –
Nothing on earth endures ...
But the love of God who sent His son
Is forever and ever yours!

Death Is A Doorway

On the "Wings of death"
    the "soul takes flight"
To the land where
    "there is no night" –
: those who believe
    what the Saviour said
Will rise in glory
    though they be dead ...
death comes to us
    just to "open the door"
the Kingdom of God
    and life evermore.
Every mile we walk in sorrow
    Brings us nearer to God's tomorrow!

Spring Awakens What Autumn Puts To Sleep

A garden of asters of varying hues,
Crimson-pinks and violet-blues,
Blossoming in the hazy Fall
Wrapped in Autumn's lazy pall –
But early frost stole in one night
And like a chilling, killing blight
It touched each pretty aster's head
And now the garden's still and dead
And all the lovely flowers that bloomed
Will soon be buried and entombed

In Winter's icy shroud of snow
But oh, how wonderful to know
That after Winter comes the Spring
To breathe new life in everything,
And all the flowers that fell in death
Will be awakened by Spring's breath –
For in God's Plan both men and flowers
Can only reach "bright, shining hours"
By dying first to rise in glory
And prove again the Easter Story.

"Because He Lives ...
We, Too, Shall Live"

$\mathcal{I}$n this restless world of struggle
        it is very hard to find
Answers to the questions
        that daily come to mind –
We cannot see the future
        what's beyond is still unknown
For the secret of God's kingdom
        still belongs to Him alone
But He granted us salvation
        when His Son was crucified
For life became immortal
        because our Saviour died.
Life is not a transient thing –
        It is *change* but never *loss*
For Christ purchased our salvation
        When He died upon the *Cross*.

Give Us Daily Awareness

On life's busy thoroughfares
We meet with angels unawares –
So, Father, make us kind and wise
So we may always recognize
The blessings that are ours to take,
The friendships that are ours to make
If we but open our heart's door wide
To let the sunshine of love inside.

When I Must Leave You

When I must leave you
    for a little while,
Please do not grieve
    and shed wild tears
And hug your sorrow
    to you through the years,
But start out bravely
    with a gallant smile;
And for my sake
    and in my name
Live on and do
    all things the same.
Feed not your loneliness
    on empty days,

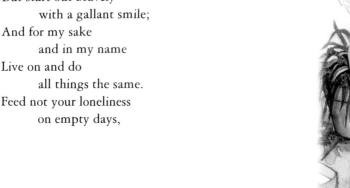

t fill each waking hour
    in useful ways,
ach out your hand
    in comfort and in cheer
d I in turn will comfort you
    and hold you near;
d never, never
    be afraid to die,
I am waiting
    for you in the sky!
part with our loved ones
    but not forever
ve trust God's promise
    and doubt it never.

Death Opens The Door
To Life Evermore

We live a short while on earth below,
Reluctant to die for we do not know
Just what "dark death" is all about
And so we view it with fear and doubt
Not certain of what is around the bend
We look on death as the final end
To all that made us a mortal being
And yet there lies just beyond our seeing
A beautiful life so full and complete
That we should leave with hurrying feet
To walk with God by sacred streams
Amid beauty and peace beyond our dreams
For all who believe in the risen Lord
Have been assured of this reward
And death for them is just "graduation"

a higher realm of wide elevation –
life on earth is a transient affair,
t a few brief years in which to prepare
r a life that is free from pain and tears
here time is not counted by hours or years –
death is only the method God chose
colonize heaven with the souls of those
ho by their apprenticeship on earth
oved worthy to dwell in the land of new birth –
death is not sad ... it's a time for elation,
joyous transition ... the soul's emigration
to a place where the soul's safe and free
live with God through Eternity!

Life Is Eternal

"Life is eternal", the good Lord said,
So do not think of your loved ones as dead –
For death is only a stepping-stone
To a beautiful life we have never known.
A place where God promised man he would be
Eternally happy and safe and free,
A wonderful land where we live anew
When our journey on earth is over and through –
So trust in God and doubt Him never
For all who love Him live forever,
And while we cannot understand
Just let the Saviour take your hand,
For when death's angel comes to call
"God is so great and we're so small" ...
And there is nothing you need fear
For faith in God makes all things clear.

God Needed An Angel In Heaven

When Jesus lived upon the earth
    so many years ago,
called the children close to Him
    because He loved them so ...
d with that tenderness of old,
    that same sweet, gentle way,
 holds your little loved one close
    within His arms today ...
d you'll find comfort in your faith
    that in His Home above
e God of little children
    gives your little one His love ...
think of your little darling
    lighthearted and happy and free
ying in God's Promised Land
    where there is joy eternally.

All Nature Proclaims Eternal Life

Flowers sleeping 'neath the snow,
Awakening when the Spring winds blow;
Leafless trees so bare before,
Gowned in lacy green once more;
Hard, unyielding, frozen sod
Now softly carpeted by God,
Still streams melting in the Spring,
Rippling over rocks that sing;
Barren, windswept, lonely hills
Turning gold with daffodils ...
These *miracles* are all around
Within our sight and touch and sound,
As true and wonderful today
As when "the stone was rolled away"
Proclaiming to all doubting men
That in God all things live again.

"I Know That My Redeemer Liveth"

They asked me how I know it's true
that the Saviour lived and died ...
And if I believe the story
that the Lord was crucified?
And I have so many answers
to prove His Holy Being,
answers that are everywhere
within the realm of seeing ...
The leaves that fell at Autumn
and were buried in the sod
now budding on the tree boughs
to lift their arms to God ...
The flowers that were covered
and entombed beneath the snow
pushing through the "darkness"
to bid the Spring "hello" ...
On every side Great Nature
retells the Easter Story –
so who am I to question
"the Resurrection Glory".

As Long As You Live And Remember – Your Loved One Lives In Your Heart!

May tender memories
        soften your grief,
May fond recollection
        bring you relief,
And may you find comfort
        and peace in the thought
Of the joy that knowing
        your loved one brought –
For time and space
        can never divide
Or keep your loved one
        from your side
When memory paints
        in colors true
The happy hours
        that belonged to you.

A Consolation Meditation

On the wings
   of death and sorrow
God sends us
   new hope for tomorrow
And in His mercy
   and His grace
He gives us strength
   to bravely face
The lonely days
   that stretch ahead
And know our loved one
   is not dead
But only sleeping
   and out of our sight
And we'll meet in that land
   Where there is no night.

In The Hands Of God Even Death Is A Time For Rejoicing

And so when death brings weeping
and the heart is filled with sorrow,
It beckons us to seek God
as we ask about "tomorrow"
And in these hours of "heart-hurt"
we draw closer to believing
That even death in God's hands
is not a cause for grieving
But a time for joy in knowing
death is just a stepping-stone
To a life that's everlasting
such as we have never known.